ANNOUNCING THE HAVERGAL EDITION
NOW IN PREPARATION FOR PUBLICATION

The edition of *The Complete Works of Frances Ridley Havergal* has five parts:

Volume I *Behold Your King: The Complete Poetical Works of Frances Ridley Havergal*

Volume II *Whose I Am and Whom I Serve: Prose Works of Frances Ridley Havergal*

Volume III *Loving Messages for the Little Ones: Works for Children by Frances Ridley Havergal*

Volume IV *Love for Love: Frances Ridley Havergal: Memorials, Letters and Biographical Works*

Volume V *Songs of Truth and Love: Music by Frances Ridley Havergal and William Henry Havergal*

David L. Chalkley, Editor   Glen T. Wegge, Music Editor

The Music of Frances Ridley Havergal by Glen T. Wegge, Ph.D.

This Companion Volume to the Havergal edition is a valuable presentation of F.R.H.'s scores, most or nearly all of F.R.H.'s scores very little if any at all seen, or even known of, for nearly a century. What a valuable body of music has been unknown for so long and is now made available to many. Dr. Wegge completed his Ph.D. in Music Theory at Indiana University at Bloomington, and his diligence and thoroughness in this volume are obvious. First an analysis of F.R.H.'s compositions is given, an essay that both addresses the most advanced musicians and also reaches those who are untrained in music; then all the extant scores that have been found are newly typeset, with complete texts for each score and extensive indices at the end of the book. This volume presents F.R.H.'s music in newly typeset scores diligently prepared by Dr. Wegge, and Volume V of the Havergal edition presents the scores in facsimile, the original 19th century scores. (The essay—a dissertation—analysing her scores is given the same both in this Companion Volume and in Volume V of the Havergal edition.)

Dr. Wegge is also preparing all of these scores for publication in performance folio editions.

Frances Ridley Havergal Trust   P.O. Box 649   Kirksville, Missouri 64501

This portrait was made in Frances' last year, when she was visiting friends in London in February, 1879 (two months or so after her 42nd birthday on December 14). There are strong reasons to think that this portrait is in no way flattering but gives an accurate copy of how she looked at that time. Ira Sankey, D. L. Moody's song leader, visited her weeks before her very unexpected early death, and he later commented on how young she looked; others also commented on how she looked younger than her age in years. Both Frances and her family would have accepted only an accurate, realistic, truthful portrait, never a flattering one. The brooch was a gift to her from her father, having Frances' personal emblem, a harp; this was one of very pieces of jewelry she kept, clearly special to her, and she had months earlier sold nearly all her other jewelry, to give the proceeds to the support of foreign missions. She was full of life and love, glowing Christ, and those who knew her or saw and heard her realized what can scarcely be conveyed on paper. In this way her sister Miriam wrote of how she sang "in quick tune, and with the spirit which only those who heard her can imagine" (from the small book *Footprints and Living Songs*, the essay on Frances' hymns by Miriam Crane). Her sister Maria was quoted in the following notice printed in the newspaper *The Christian* for July 3, 1879: "THE LATE MISS F. RIDLEY HAVERGAL.—Mr. T. J. Hughes, of 2 Elm Row, Hampstead [London], has shown us a portrait in chalk for which Miss Havergal sat to him several times. This likeness is recommended by her sister, Miss M. V. G. Havergal, as being so life-like. Orders for photographic copies, at a guinea each, may be sent to Mr. Hughes."

ART SONGS

COMPOSED BY

Frances Ridley Havergal.

Edited by Glen T. Wegge, Ph.D.

An urtext score from the 19th century published scores.

Copyright © 2012 Frances Ridley Havergal Trust. All rights are reserved.
Frances Ridley Havergal Trust P.O.Box 649 Kirksville, Missouri 63501

ISBN 978-1-937236-47-2
Library of Congress Control Number: 2014916035

Printed in the United States of America
This book is printed on acid-free paper.
All rights are reserved by Glen T. Wegge, Ph.D.

In the early part of the 21st century, comparatively few people recognize the name Frances Ridley Havergal, and among those who do, she is best known for her hymns, that is, her words sung in hymns. For the past 100 years or so, few have realized that she was a composer, leaving important, valuable scores. In the last six or eight years of her life, and in the 20 or 25 years after her death, she was very widely known and highly regarded on both sides of the Atlantic, known for her poetry and prose. She was also a very richly gifted musician, a fine pianist, singer, and composer. This folio contains all of her arts songs that have been found.

F.R.H. was a rarely gifted musician and composer. The researcher of the Havergal edition, David Chalkley, has said that Frances in her musical gifts was at the level of the three finest lady composers that he knows of, Fanny Mendelssohn Hensel, Clara Wieck Schumann, and Cecile Chaminade, but she never concentrated fully on music as those three had the opportunity to do. This does not mean that she did not concentrate seriously on music (both performance and composition): she was very diligent, and truly, deeply loved music (she was a true musician to the core), only music was not the top priority of time, attention, and effort in her life. Ferdinand Hiller (now very much forgotten, but in his day regarded with Brahms as the two foremost German composers after Mendelssohn and Schumann died), a truly brilliant musician and composer, was deeply impressed with Frances' scores that he sightread in her presence, and he readily offered to teach her himself. Several others, very advanced musicians in her day, recognized her special gifts and made strong comments about her as a composer. Her harmony was very special. Her scores are similar to her poetry in this way: there are ones that are very easy to grasp, very accessible, showing child-like wonder (though true art shows or presents the most sublime and artistic as simple, easy, natural), and others that are extremely sophisticated, showing very deep knowledge of music. As a composer, she had an early period and a middle period (showing her own clear voice, sophisticated music), but she died at 42 and a half, before a third, late period as a composer. Her scores are very advanced, compositionally very fine, full of advanced technical knowledge, creative invention, insight, life, beauty.

So much more could be said. Here are two examples, among so many others: Years before Gustav Mahler did this, she used nonconcentric tonality within a movement (not including change of key in anticipation of or transition to the next section or movement). She often used a chromatic third relationship in her harmony, which is very Romantic. T. H. Darlow in his brief biography of F.R.H. (written very much with the collaboration of Frances' nephew Alfred Havergal Shaw, and her niece Frances Anna Shaw, both of whom knew her well), wrote this: "She had no keener pleasure than to render on the piano the best of Bach, Handel, Haydn, Beethoven, Mendelssohn, Schumann, and Schubert." (*Frances Ridley Havergal: A Saint of God* by Thomas Herbert Darlow, London: James Nisbet & Co., 1927, original book pages 17–18, page 1096 of Volume IV of the Havergal edition)

Many important details on F.R.H. are given in Volume V of the Havergal edition, *Songs of Truth and Love: Music by Frances Ridley Havergal and William Henry Havergal*, and in the Companion Volume *The Music of Frances Ridley Havergal*, much, very valuable information on her as a pianist, singer, and composer, truly important details on her as a musician and on her compositions that remain extant today. Both books are virtually ready for the printers at this time, and, if the Lord wills, are to be published soon.

This performance folio is based on the previously mentioned Volume V of the definitive edition of *The Complete Works of Frances Ridley Havergal*, and on the Companion Volume to the edition, *The Music of Frances Ridley Havergal*. Her manuscript scores have been found for only four of these art songs ("Whom having not seen, ye love," "That's Not the Way at Sea," "God bless the boys of England," and "Begin at Once"), but the first edition scores are definitive, and this is an urtext edition of those 19th century published scores.

Although Frances' music became very obscure (almost completely forgotten, with likely very few if any having seen or performed these scores in the past 50 or 75 or 100 years), this is a rich, valuable body of music, truly to the Lord's glory and the good of His people.

In the Prefatory Note to the posthumously published *Loyal Responses* with music (another volume of F.R.H.'s music, also to be published in a folio performance edition similar to this one), her sister Maria V. G. Havergal quoted these words by Frances: "Why put off joyous singing till we reach the happier shore? Let us sing words which we feel and love, with clearness of enunciation, and looking up to meet His smile all the while we are singing. So shall we loyally sing for our King, yes for Him, Whose voice is our truest music."

Thanks be to God for His indescribable gift to us in Christ.

Glen T. Wegge, Ph.D.

Contents

Note: The words and music are by F.R.H. unless otherwise specified.

These next seven quotations are taken from the edition of *The Complete Works of Frances Ridley Havergal*.

[F.R.H.'s sister Maria Vernon Graham Havergal wrote this in *Memorials of Frances Ridley Havergal* (London: James Nisbet & Co., 1880), original book pages 79–80, page 24 of Volume IV of the Havergal edition.]

It may not be out of place here to mention that such was the strength of her musical memory, that she would play through Handel, much of Beethoven and Mendelssohn, without any notes. A pupil of Beethoven thought her rendering of the Moonlight Sonata perfect; her touch was instinct with soul, as also was her singing.

During her stay at Oakhampton her brother-in-law engaged Dr. Wm. Marshall to give her singing lessons; and she attended the meetings of the Philharmonic Society at Kidderminster, of which he was the conductor. The practice of sacred music was an extreme gratification to her, and she soon became a valued solo singer. Her rendering of Mendelssohn's "Woe unto them," "But the Lord is mindful of His own," are remembered as peculiarly effective, though it was in Handel's music that she more particularly delighted.

[*Swiss Letters and Alpine Poems* was a posthumous book of F.R.H.'s letters written during stays in Switzerland, edited and published by F.R.H.'s sister Miriam Crane. Her sister Maria wrote this about Frances in Chapter XIII "Memoranda of a Swiss Tour with F.R.H. by Her Sister M.V.G.H., in *Swiss Letters and Alpine Poems* (London: James Nisbet & Co., 1881), original book pages 86–87, page 361 of Volume IV of the Havergal edition.]

At Champéry the delightful ministrations of Mr. Rogers, the chaplain, new friendships, and Frances' incessant ministries, whether by song, or conversation, or Bible reading, filled up every day. One evening, after playing the Moonlight Sonata, an aged German lady assured me that it quite recalled Beethoven's own rendering of it.

[This may be the "pupil of Beethoven" referred to in the first paragraph of the previous quotation, who thought Frances' "rendering of the Moonlight Sonata perfect" (in *Memorials* by Maria). Note: This account in Switzerland was dated August 10, 1876. Beethoven had died 49 years earlier, so that if this woman was, for example, 25 when Beethoven died, she would have been 74 when she heard F.R.H.]

[F.R.H.'s sister Maria wrote this about Frances in *The Aubiography of Maria Vernon Graham* (London: James Nisbet & Co., 1887), original book pages 86–87, page 515 of Volume IV of the Havergal edition. Cecilia was their niece, the daughter of their brother Henry East Havergal.]

Then how delicious Fan's touch on the pianette she bought specially for me! Sometimes rapid waves of melody, rising, falling, ebbing into softest ripple, then full glorious chords, so reminding me of dear father's harmonies. Often she sang for me her recitative and air to the words in Isaiah 12: "And in that day thou shalt say, O Lord, I will praise Thee: though Thou wast angry with me, Thine anger is turned away, and Thou comfortedest me." Then a brilliant, "Behold, God is my salvation; I will trust, and not be afraid,"—the very shout of a victor. But the third verse, "Therefore with joy shall ye draw water out of the wells of salvation," was real water music, the notes seemed sparkles of water dropping gladly, and the illusion was so perfect that one's soul seemed refreshingly sprayed with joy! Alas! that priceless manuscript is lost. Frances had written it all down within a few days of her death. I believe my sister told me she had sent it to some critic. I have inquired and searched vainly for this "my lost chord." The melody floats through and through me still, yet strangely I cannot sing it. Dear Cecilia is the only one who remembers somewhat of its melody.

[Next is an excerpt from an essay on F.R.H.'s hymns by her sister, Jane Miriam Crane, in *Footprints and Living Songs* (London: Home Words Publishing Office, date uncertain, ? 1883), original book pages 57–59, page 888 of Volume IV of the Havergal edition. Miriam was 19 when Frances was born, and lived 19 years after Frances died.]

Her ardent missionary zeal, now commemorated by "the Frances Ridley Havergal Church Missionary Memorial Fund," is exemplified in her animated and eloquent "Tell it out!" which is now often sung by assembled thousands. It was written at Winterdyne one snowy Sunday morning when unable to go to church. As she afterwards said: "In reading the Psalms for the day I came to 'Tell it out among the heathen that the Lord is King,' and I thought, what a splendid first line! and then words and music came rushing in to me." When the churchgoers returned, hymn and harmonies were all beautifully written out, and then sung, in quick tune, and with the spirit which only those who heard her can imagine.

[Next is an excerpt from Frances Ridley Havergal *Worcestershire Hymnwriter* by Janet Grierson (Worcestershire: The Havergal Society, 1879), original book pages 167–168, pages 1209–1210 of Volume IV of the Havergal edition. The regular paragraphs are Miss Grierson's words, and the indented paragraph is Miss Grierson's quotation of F.R.H.]

Early in February 1879 Frances spent a fortnight in London. The main object of her visit was to see her publishers, Mr. Watson and Mr. Robertson of Nisbet & Co., and Mr. Hutchings and Mr. Romer who were the publishers of her music. . . . . It was partly on the Rev. S. G. Prout's account that she went to see Mr. Hutchings and Mr. Romer, as she was hoping to negotiate the publication of his verses "Loving all along," set to her own music. To her delight they approved the suggestion, and also welcomed a number of her own hymns and tunes. She describes to Maria the successful outcome of her visit:

I had a most interesting afternoon, half business, half pleasure. Both of them were taken with "Tell it out," and think it "such a hit," etc., and are going to issue it at once in song form, as solo and chorus with piano accompaniment. Then they wanted more of the same, and I sang my tunes "Euodias" to " 'Tis the church triumphant," and "Onesimus" to "Only for Thee," and "Hermas" to "Golden harps are sounding," and others; and they wish me to prepare a whole set. They say, "Tell it out" is safe to go. Mr. R. had never heard me play any sacred music before, and he started up, and said, "Ha! you are mistress here!" He exceedingly admires "When thou passest," and is going to publish it.

Since the account of this performance comes from the artiste herself, it is interesting to note that it appears to tally with what others have said of her musical prowess. A. W. Baldwin in "The Macdonald Sisters," basing his account on Edith Macdonald's diary, records that "There used to be prayer meetings at Bewdley, as elsewhere, and these were especially distinguished by the attendance of Frances Ridley Havergal. This accomplished lady would spring to the harmonium, grasp the notes as if they were alive, and passionately sing her own moving hymns."

———————————

[This is part of a letter that F.R.H. wrote to James Parlane in 1876, found in *Letters by the Late Frances Ridley Havergal* (London: James Nisbet & Co., 1885), original book pages 265–266, pages 221–222 of Volume IV of the Havergal edition. Her phrase "Ministry of Song" refers to her first published book, *The Ministry of Song*, which is also the title of the second poem in that book, "The Ministry of Song." She was a wonderfully gifted pianist, and she accompanied herself on the piano.]

. . . I must tell you a wonderful bit of Ministry of Song, through "Whom having not seen, ye love." I was taken on speculation to call on a clever young gentleman, just an infidel, knowing the Bible and disbelieving it, and believing that nobody else really believes, but that religion is all humbug and mere profession. I was not primed at all, only knew that he was "not a religious man." In the first place, I had no end of fun with him, and got on thoroughly good terms—then was asked to sing. I prayed the whole time I was singing, and felt God very near and helping me. After a Handel song or two which greatly delighted him, I sang "Tell it out!" felt the glorious truth that He is King, and couldn't help breaking off in the very middle and saying so, right out!

Then I sang, "Whom having not seen, ye love," and felt as if could sing out all the love of my heart in it. Well, this young infidel, who had seemed extremely surprised and subdued by "Tell it out," competely broke down, and went away to hide his tears in a bay window. And afterwards we sat down together, and he let me "tell it out" as I pleased, and it was not hard to speak of Him of whom I had sung. He seemed altogether struck and subdued, and listened like a child. He said, "Well there is faith then, you have it anyhow—I saw it when you sang, and could not stand it, and that's the fact!" He was anxious for me to come again.

When I came away, his sister, who had introduced me, wept for joy, saying she had persuaded me to come with a vague hope that he "might find he could tolerate a religious person," but never dared to hope such an effect as this, and that she thought I had been most marvellously guided in drawing the bow at a venture, for every word and even action had been just right. I tell you this just because you are publishing both "Tell it out" and other leaflets for me. Will you sometimes pray that God's especial blessing will go with them? I should add that it was almost a miracle in another way, for I had such a wretched cold that I doubted being able to sing at all, and yet I believe I never sang clearer and better and stronger. How good God is!

———————————

[Next is part of a letter that F.R.H. wrote in 1869 to John Spencer Curwen, the leader of the Tonic Sol-fa movement, a letter full of such rich truth, found in *Letters by the Late Frances Ridley Havergal* (London: James Nisbet & Co., 1885), original book pages 68–69, page 165 of Volume IV of the Havergal edition. "Stay and think," think on the last phrase: the One name which is sweeter than any music. Writing of the benefit to girls who attended Tonic Sol-fa lessons being taught, Frances wrote this:

. . . . My chief reason for adopting it with them instead of the established notation was that all the Sol-fa songs are sound and safe, and I knew I could not give them access to anything low or bad through it, while I had no such certainty had I taught the old notation. . . . . There was no question as to the class being attractive, and great was the disappointment when, as frequently happened, the members were kept at work too late and "lost the singing."

One evening two girls came in panting and flushed, about fifteen minutes before the close. "Why Lizzie and Jane, what is the matter?" "We were kept overtime, but we thought half a loaf better than no bread, so we took to our heels the moment we could get out of the workroom, and we never stopped running till we got here." They had literally run a good mile to be in time for a few minutes' singing.

One young girl who had just begun to form acquaintances which would have led to no good, and to saunter about the streets with them, was attracted to our rooms solely by the singing class, but soon became one of our most regular attendants at all the classes, and we have reason to hope that she is not only saved from the dangers into which she was rushing, but that good impressions have been made, and a good work begun in her heart. I have no musical results to show, for after about eight lessons I was interrupted by illness, but I believe that my Tonic Sol-fa class had been a grappling iron to draw many little drifting vessels close to our side, bringing them within hearing of loving and sympathising words, and of the One name which is sweeter than any music.

These seven quotations are a glimpse, and much more could be said, statements by F.R.H. and accounts by those who knew her or heard her.

The first couplet of the Consecration Hymn and her signsture.

Whom having not seen, ye love.

Recitative and Air.

By Frances Ridley Havergal.

Recitative. (I Pet. 1. 5-7.)

Who are kept through the power of God by faith unto salvation,

ready to be revealed in the last time. Wherein ye greatly re-

joice, though now, for a season, if need be, if need be,

Whom Having Not Seen, Ye Love

Recitative and Air

I Peter 1: 5-8

Words in I Peter 1: 5-8
Music by Frances Ridley Havergal

Who are kept by the pow'r of God through faith un-to sal-

va-tion, rea-dy to be re-veal-èd in the last time:___ Where in ye great-ly re-

joice, though now for a sea-son, if need be, if need be,

ye are in hea-vi-ness through man-i-fold temp-ta-tions; That the

tri-al of your faith, be-ing much more pre-cious than of gold that per-ish-eth,

though it be tried with__ fire, might be found un-to praise, and hon-our, and glo - ry, at the ap - pear - ing of Je - sus Christ.

a tempo

rall.

Air   I Pet. 1: 8.

Whom hav-ing not seen, ye love; Whom

Air

ha ving not seen, ye love; in Whom, though now ye see Him not, yet be-

30 liev-ing, ye re-joice ___ though now ye see Him not,   though

35 now, ___ though now ye see Him not,   ye see Him

40 not. Yet be - liev - ing, be - liev - ing, be - liev ing ye ___ re - joice, ___ re-

45
p pp
joice with joy, with joy un - speak-a ble, un-
Pno.
8vb
50
f
speak-a-ble, and full of glo - ry, and full of glo - ry,
Pno.
55
p f
with joy un-speak-a ble, and full of glo - ry, and full, full of
Pno.

glo - - - ry.

Whom hav ing not seen, ye love, Whom ha-ving not seen, ye

love, In Whom, though now ye see Him not, yet be - liev-ing, ye re-

73
f
rall.
joice, ye re - joice, yet be - liev - ing ye re-
Pno.
f
rall.
8vb
78
joice.
a tempo
(8vb)
82
8vb

Loving All Along

Sacred Song

Music by Frances Ridley Havergal
Words by S. Gillespie Prout

1.Tramp,   tramp on the down-ward   way, With sel-dom a   stop and ne-ver a

stay,   Lov ing the dark-ness, ha-ting   light, Our fa - ces   set to wards e-ter - nal night! Each has ans-wered God's cry, "Why will ye die?

Turn ye! turn ye!" "Not I, not I!" We have

bar - tered a-way His__ gems and gold For the emp - ty husks and the sha - dows cold; We have laugh'd at the De - mon's tight - 'ning chains, And

bid - den him forge them strong! And God has kept on lov - ing us,

Lov ing, all__ a - long! And God has kept on lov - ing us, Lov - ing, all along!

Tempo primo
con espressione

2.The___   Love still fol - lows as
3.And the   ten - der voice___ pur-

we tramp on; A sor - row - ful fall in its plead - ing tone; "Thou wilt
sues each one: "My Child,___ what more could thy God have done? Thy___

tire in the drea - ry ways of sin; I___ left My___ home to
sin hid the light of Heav'n from Me, When a - lone in the dark - ness I

48   rall.

bring thee in! In its gold - en___ street Stand__ no wea - ry
died for thee! Thy__ sin of this day, In its sha - dow__

Pno.

rall.

52

feet, Its rest is glor - ious, its songs are___ sweet!"
lay Be - tween My face___ and One turn'd a - way!"

Pno.

Ped.

57   Allegro

And we shout back an - gri - ly, hurry - ing on To a
And we stop and turn for a mo - ment's space, Fling - ing

Pno.

Allegro

✻

ter - ri - ble home where___ rest is none: "We want not your Ci - ty's__
back__ the love in the Sa - viour's face, To give His__ heart yet a-

Chorus
Andante
ad. lib.

gild - ed street Nor to hear its con stant song!" And still God keeps on
no - ther grief, And__ glo - ry in the wrong! And Christ is al - ways

Chorus
Andante
ad. lib.

lov - ing us, Loving, all__ a - long, And still God keeps on lov - ing us,
lov - ing us, Loving, all__ a - long, And Christ is al - ways lov - ing us,

Tempo primo

72

Lov - ing, all a - long!
Lov - ing, all a - long!

4.One is bend ing low be-

Pno.

Tempo primo

77

fore the King, And the An - gels lis - ten with quiv - 'ring wing, He has

Pno.

80

en - tered the Ci - ty and sings its hymn, While the gold of its streets thro'

Pno.

tears is dim! "To Him who so loved me and washed me white, To

Him be all hon-our and pow'r and might!" That mar - vel-lous

love No sin could___ move, Wait - ed and wear-ied not,

sought　and　strove!　To＿ us through the dark ness, the　Voice still calls From the

gleam-ing heights of the　jas-per walls; To the　long kept pla-ces our　wel come waits, A-

mid the exul ting　throng.　And　God will still be　lov - ing us,　Lov ing　all＿ along, And God will still be lov - ing us, Lov - ing, all a-

long! Lov - ing, all a - long! Lov - ing, all a - long!

Precious Blood
Sacred Song

Tune-Urbane II
Andante

Words and Music by
Frances Ridley Havergal

1.Pre - cious, pre - cious Blood of Je - sus, Shed on Cal - va - ry,
2.Though thy sins are red like crim - son, Deep in scar - let glow,

Shed for re - bels, shed for sin - ners, Shed for thee!_____
Je - su's pre - cious blood shall make thee White as snow!_____

Pre - cious, pre - cious Blood of Je - sus, Let it make thee whole!
Pre - cious blood that hath re-deem'd us! All the price is paid!

Let it flow in migh - ty cleans - ing O'er thy soul.____
Per - fect par - don now is of - fer'd, Peace is made.____

Chorus

Pre - cious, pre - cious Blood of Je - sus, E - ver flow - ing free____ O be-lieve it,

O re-ceive it, 'Tis for thee!

Only for Thee

Tune-Onesimus
Smoothly & Cheerfully

Music by Frances Ridley Havergal
Words by E. A. Walker

1.Pre - cious Sa - viour, may I live, On - ly for Thee!
2.Be my smiles and be my tears, On - ly for Thee!

Spend the pow - ers Thou dost give, On - ly for Thee!
Be my young and ri - per years, On - ly for Thee!

Be my spi-rit's deep de-sire, On-ly for
Be my peace and be my strife, On-ly for

Thee! May my in-tel-lect as-pire, On-ly for Thee!
Thee! Be my love and be my life, On-ly for Thee!

In my joys may I re-joice, On-ly for
Be my song and be my sigh, On-ly for

Thee! In my choic - es make my choice, On - ly for
Thee! Let me live and let me die, On - ly for

Thee! Meek-ly may I suf-fer grief, On - ly for
Thee! Be my ris - ing, be my glo-ry, On - ly for

Thee! Grate - ful - ly ac - cept re - lief, On - ly for
Thee! Be my whole e - ter - ni - ty, On - ly for

Thee!   On – ly for Thee!
Thee!   On – ly for Thee!

Pno.

Golden Harps
Sacred Song

Words and Music by
Frances Ridley Havergal

Tune-Hermas

Joyously

1.Gol - den Harps are sound - ing,   An - gel voi - ces ring,
2.He who came to save us,   He who bled and died,

Pear - ly gates are o - pen'd, O - pen'd for the
Now is crown'd with glo - ry, At His Fa - ther's

King. Christ, the King of Glo - ry, Je - sus, King of
side. Ne - ver more to suf - fer, Ne - ver more to

Love, Is gone up in tri - umph, To His throne a -
die, Je - sus, King of Glo - ry, Is gone up on

bove.
high.

All His work is end - ed, Joy - ful - ly we

sing, Je - sus hath as - cend - ed! Glo - ry to our

King.

Tell It Out
Sacred Song

Tune-Epenetus

With Spirit

Words and Music by
Frances Ridley Havergal

1. Tell it out a-mong the hea-then that the Lord is King! Tell it
2. Tell it out a-mong the hea-then that the Sa - viour reigns! Tell it

out! Tell it out! Tell it out among the na - tions, bid them
out! Tell it out! Tell it out among the na - tions, bid them

shout and sing. Tell it out!   Tell it out.   Tell it
burst their chains. Tell it out!   Tell it out.   Tell it

Slower, with Expression

out with a - dor - a - tion that He shall in - crease; That the
out a - mong the weep - ing ones that Je - sus lives; Tell it

might - y King of Glo - ry is the King of Peace; Tell it
out a - mong the wea - ry ones what rest He gives: Tell it

Lyrics beneath staves:

17
out with ju - bil - a - tion though the waves may roar, That He
out a - mong the sin - ners that He came to save; Tell it

19
sit - teth on the wa - ter - floods, our King for e - ver - more. Tell it
out a - mong the dy - ing that He tri - umphed o'er the grave. Tell it

Chorus

21
out a mong the hea-then that the Lord is King! Tell it out! Tell it
out a mong the hea-then that the Sa - viour reigns! Tell it out! Tell it

out! Tell it out among the na-tions, bid them shout and sing! Tell it
out! Tell it out among the na-tions, bid them burst their chains! Tell it

out! Tell it out!
out! Tell it out!

Tell it out among the heathen Jesus reigns above!

  Tell it out! Tell it out!

Tell it out among the nations that His reigns in love!

  Tell it out! Tell it out!

Tell it out among the highways and the lanes at home:

Let it ring across the mountains and the ocean foam!

Like the sound of many waters let our glad shout be,

Till it echo and re-echo from the islands of the sea!

Resting
Sacred Song

Words and Music by
Frances Ridley Havergal

1.Rest ing on the faith - ful - ness of Christ___ our Lord,
2.Rest ing in the life - boat while the waves___ roll high,

Rest-ing on the ful - ness of___ His own sure Word,___
Rest-ing in the for - tress while___ the foe is nigh;___

Rest - ing   on   His   pow'r,   on   His   love   un - told,
Rest - ing   in   the   chariot   for   the   swift   glad   race;

Pno.

Rest - ing   on   His   co - ve - nant   se - cured____ of   old.
Rest - ing,   al - ways   rest - ing   in   His   bound - less   grace.

Pno.

3. Rest - ing 'neath His   guid - ing Hand for   un - track-èd   days;
4. Rest - ing   in   the   pas - tures, and be - neath____ the   Rock;

Pno.

Rest - ing 'neath His sha - dow from the noon - tide rays;
Rest - ing by the wa - ters where He leads His flock;

Rest - ing at the e - ven - tide be - neath His wing,
Rest - ing, while we lis - ten, at His glo - rious feet,

In the fair pa - vi - lion of our Sa - viour King.
Rest - ing in His ve - ry arms, O rest com - plete!

Rest-ing,   rest - ing   with   Christ_____ our   King,
Rest-ing,   rest - ing,   O   Rest_____ com -   plete!

Rest-ing,   rest - ing   with   Christ   our   King.
rest - ing,   rest - ing,   O   Rest   com -   plete!

5. Rest-ing and be-liev-ing, let us on - ward press;

Rest-ing in Him - self,___ the Lord___ our Righ - teous - ness!

Rest-ing and re - joic - ing, let___ His saved ones sing,

Glo - ry, glo - ry, glo - ry be to Christ____ our King.

Glo - ry,   glo - ry to Christ____ our King!

Glo - ry,   glo - ry to Christ____ our King!

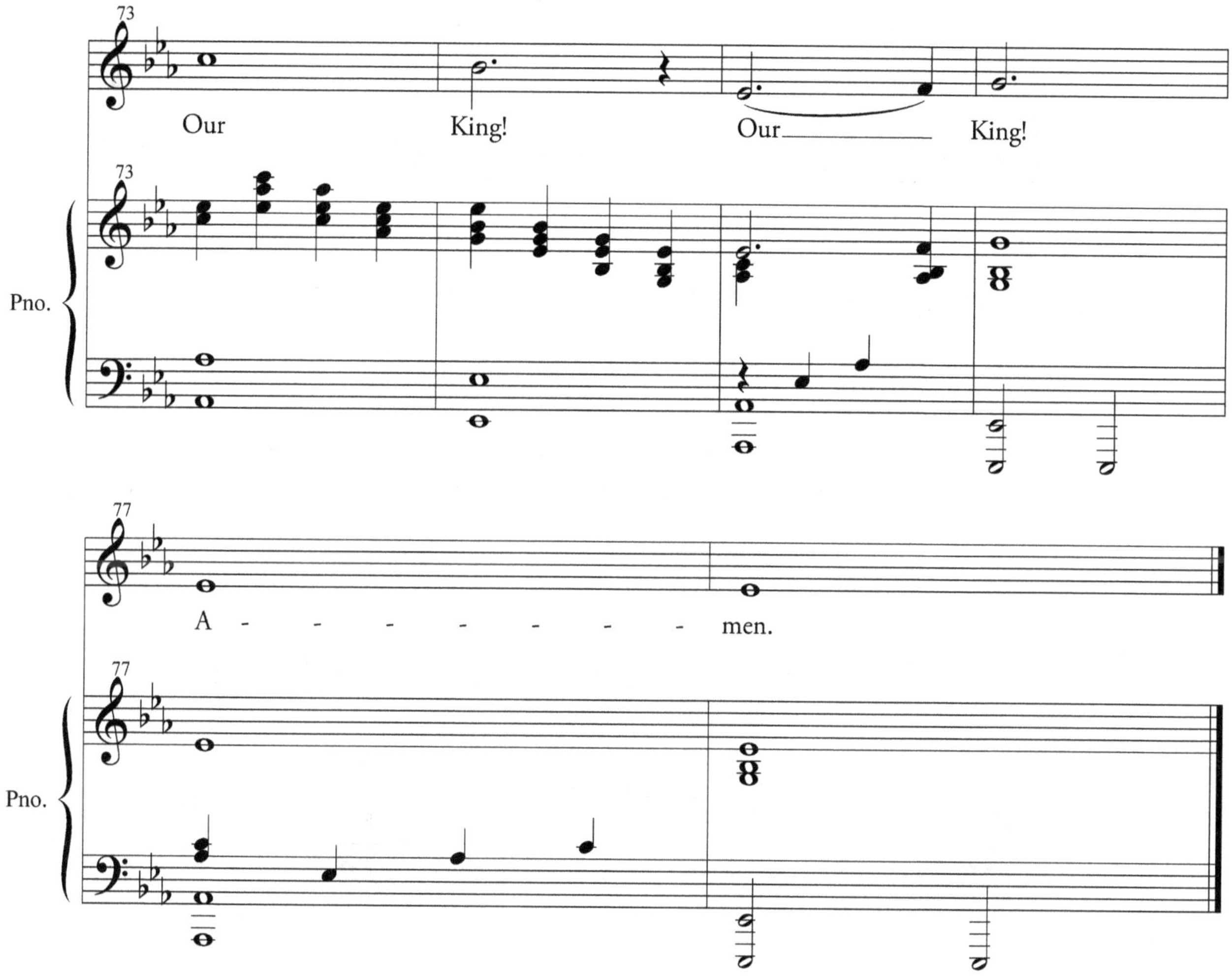
73
Our
King!
Our
King!
73
Pno.
77
A - - - - - - - men.
77
Pno.

One by One
Sacred Song

Music byFrances Ridley Havergal
Words by Barbara Miller McAndrews

Lyrics (measures 8+): In se-cret love, the Mas-ter To each one whis-pers low:

"I am at hand, work fas - ter! Be - hold, the sun - set glow!" And

each one smil - eth sweet Who hears the Mas-ter's feet.

Not sweep-ing up to - geth-er In whirl-wind or in cloud, In the hush of sum-mer wea-ther, Or when storms are thun-d'ring loud: But

one by one we go, In the sweet-ness none may know. Not

press - ing through the por-tals Of that Ce-les - tial Town, An

39
ff
pp
ar - my of fresh Im - mor - tals, By the Lord of Bat - tles won; But
Pno.
43
f
ff
pp
whe - ther, Or when, storms are thun - d'ring loud; But one by one we
Pno.
47
f
go, In the sweet - ness none may know. Not press - ing through the
Pno.
Ped.

por - tals Of that Ce - les - tial Town, An ar - my of fresh Im-

mor - tals, By the Lord of Bat - tles won; But one by one we

come, To the gate of the Heav'n-ly Home. That to *each* the voice of the

63
mp
Fa-ther May thrill in wel-come sweet; And round each the an - gels
Pno.
mp
Ped.
67
f
ga - ther With songs on the shin - ing street; As
Pno.
f
70
one by one we go, To the glo - ry none may know,
Pno.
Ped.

One   by   one!   One   by   one!

When Thou Passest

Sacred Song

Isaiah 43: 1-3

Words in Isaiah 43: 1-3
Music by Frances Ridley Havergal

Recitative

Voice

Piano

Thus saith the Lord, thy Cre - a - tor, and He that form-èd thee, O

Is - ra-el: "Fear not, fear not, for I have re - deem - èd thee:

thou art Mine!"

Air

Lyrics:
When thou pas-sest through the wa-ters, I will be with thee;
when thou pas-sest through the ri-vers, they shall not o'er - flow thee;
When thou walk-est through the fire, — thou shalt not be burn - èd,

thou shalt not be burn - èd; Nei - ther shall the flame, nei - ther

shall the flame, nei - ther shall the flame,_____ kin - dle up - on thee.

When thou pas - sest through the wa - ters I will be with thee,

I will be with thee. For I am the Lord, the

Lord thy God; the Ho - ly One of Is - ra-el, the Ho - ly One, thy

Briskly and with Spi

Sa - viour, thy___ Sa - viour, thy___ Sa - viour. I gave

54
E - gypt — for thy ran som, I gave E - gypt — for thy ran som, E - thi - o - pi - a and
Pno.
59
Se - ba for thee; I gave E - gypt — for thy ran som, I gave E - gypt — for thy
Pno.
64
f
ff
ran-som, for thy ran-som, E - thi - o - pi - a and Se - ba for thee.
Pno.
8vb

When thou pas - sest through the wa - ters I will be with thee;

when thou pas - sest through the ri - vers they shall not o'er - flow thee;

When thou walk - est through the fire___ thou shalt not be burn - èd,

81
mp
thou shalt not be burn - èd; Nei - ther shall the flame, nei - ther
Pno.
mp
85
f
shall the flame, nei-ther shall the flame, kin - dle up - on thee.
Pno.
f
90
When thou pas - sest through the wa - ters I will be with thee;
Pno.

when thou pas - sest through the ri - vers I will be with thee, __

I will be with thee, ____ with __ thee.

Breast the Wave

Based on the tune St. Silas II

With Spirit and Emphasis

Music by Frances Ridley Havergal
Words by Joseph Stammers, 1830

1.Breast the wave, Chris-tian, When it is
2.Fight the fight, Chris-tian, Je - sus is

strong - est; Watch for day, Chris - tian, When the night's long - est.
o'er thee; Run the race, Chris - tian, Heav'n is be - fore thee.

On - ward and up - ward still Be thine en - dea-vour; The rest that re-
He who hath pro - mis - èd Fal - ter - eth ne - ver; The love of e-

main - eth Will be for e - ver!
- ter ni - ty Flows on for e - ver!   2.Fight the fight,
                                                3.Lift   the eye,

Christian, Just as it clos eth; Raise the heart Chris-tian, Ere it re - po seth.

Thee from the love of Christ No - thing shall se - ver! Mount when thy work is done, Praise Him for - e - ver!

A Merrie Christmas and a Happy New Year

Words and music by
Frances Ridley Havergal

birth. ___ So we keep ___ the old - en

greet - - - ing ___ With its mean - ing deep ___ and

true ___ And wish ___ "a Mer - rie Christmas, And a hap-py____ New Year____ to you."_____ A

mer rie,   mer rie Christ - mas And a hap py New Year to   you!___ A

hap py New Year to   you!____   A__ mer - rie, mer - rie Christ - mas,   A mer - rie, mer - rie Christ - mas, A hap - py New Year __ to you, ___ A

hap py New Year to you! ___ Oh! yes! A mer - rie

Christ - mas! With __ blith - est song and smile ___ With bright - est thought of

Him who dwelt, with bright-est thought of Him who dwelt, On__ earth a lit-tle

while.__ That we__ might dwell__ for

ev - - er,__ Where ne - ver falls__ a tear:__

Lyrics:
So "a Mer - rie Christ - mas to____ you," And a
hap - py,____ a hap - - py year!_____ A
mer - rie, mer - rie Christ - mas, And a hap-py New Year to you!____ A

hap-py New Year to you!___ A___ mer - rie, mer - rie Christ - mas, A

mer - rie, mer - rie Christ - mas, A hap-py New Year___ to you!___ A

hap-py New Year to you!_____

The Pilgrim's Song

Words by Friedrich La Motte-Fouqué
Music by Frances Ridley Havergal

When death is com-ing   near,   When thy heart shrinks in   fear

And   thy limbs__ fail;   Then   raise thy   hands and pray

To Him who smoothes thy way Through the dark vale

Seest thou the east - ern dawn?

Hear'st thou in the red morn, The

an - - - gels' song?

Oh lift thy droop - ing head,

Thou who in gloom and dread, Hast lain so long!

Death comes to set thee free, Oh meet him cheer - i -ly As

thy true friend; And all thy fears shall cease,

And in e - ter - nal peace, Thy sor - rows end, Thy

sor - rows end.

Dream-Singing

Words and Music by
Frances Ridley Havergal

I dreamt that I was sing-ing,   Sing-ing all for

thee,   And   still   the   notes   went   ring-ing   Far   o - ver   land   and

sea,   Far   o - ver   land   and   sea.   Went   ring-ing   till   they

found   thee,   Though   so   far   a - way,   And   soft - ly   float - ing round   thee,   Made   mu - sic   all   the   day,   all   the   day_____

_____ Made   mu - sic___   all_____   the   day.

Made   mu - sic   that   could

cheer thee, Full of gen - tle glee, Then leav - ing e - choes

near thee came back a - gain to me_____ Came

back with love and bless - ing On their spi - rit wings, With mu - si-cal ex - press - ing   Of   sweet and ho - ly things,   Of

sweet and ho - ly   things.   I dreamt that I   was   sing-ing!

Come a - gain   to   me!   And all its fai - ry ring-ing   No more a dream shall be, No more a dream, No more a dream, No

more a dream shall be.

Twilight Voices

Words and Music by
Frances Ridley Havergal

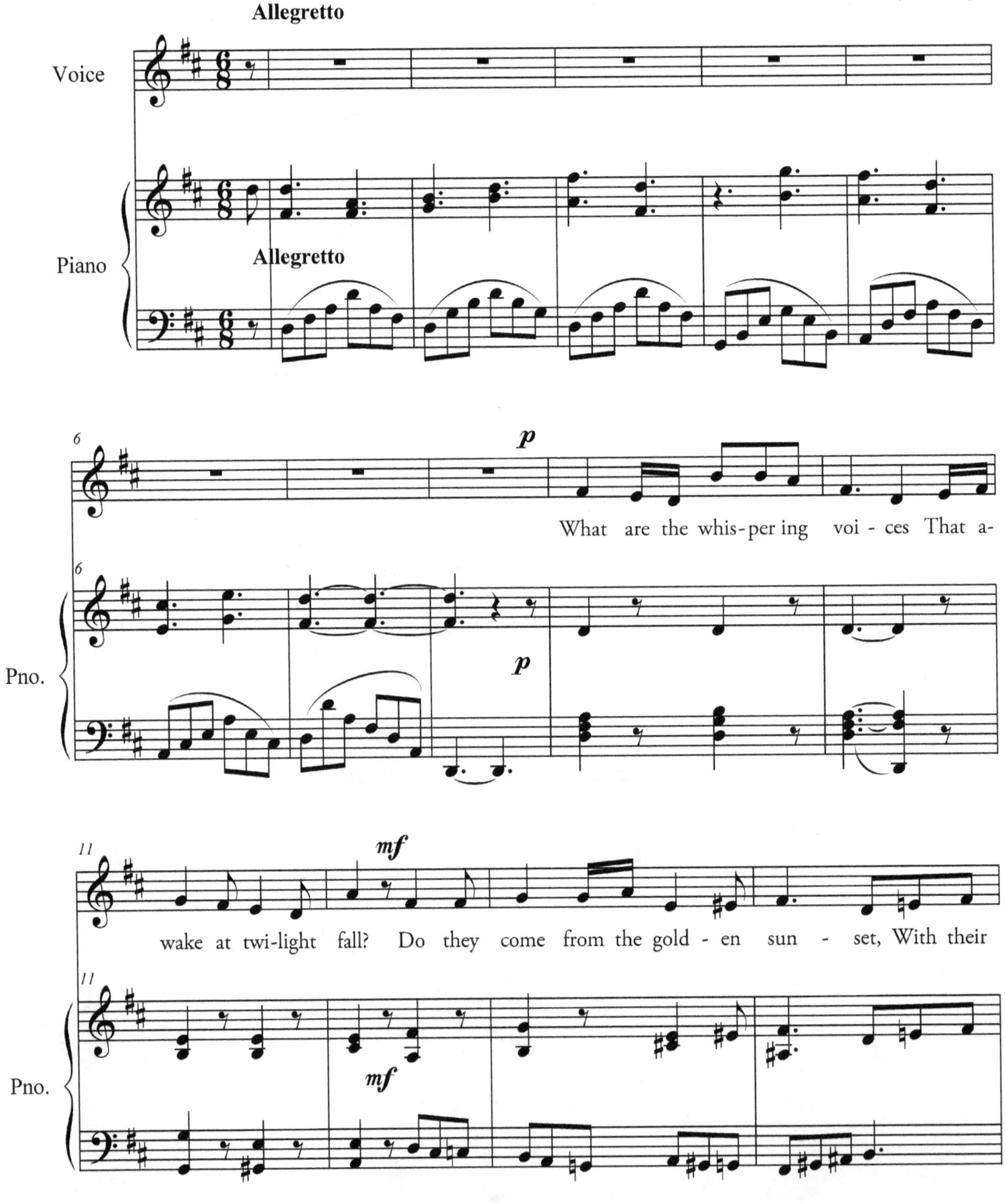
Allegretto
Voice
Piano
Allegretto
6
p
What are the whis-per ing voi - ces That a-
6
Pno.
p
11
mf
wake at twi-light fall? Do they come from the gold - en sun - set, With their
11
Pno.
mf

15
haunt - ing, haunt - ing call?
Their
Pno.
8va
leggieramente
19
haunt - ing, haunt - ing call?
Andante
They
(8va)
tr
rall.
Andante
23
tell me of bree - zy spring times, And of dream - y sum - mer
sim.

eves,　　　And of snow-wreaths mer-ri-ly　shak - en　From the

shi - ning i - vy　leaves.　　　But the

far　off　tre-ble　chang - eth　To a　ten - or　tone,　and

so, I know that the voic - es tell me

On - ly of long __ a - go, On-ly of long a - go. __ I

hear __ you, I hear you, In the gen - tle twi - light fall. __

Come to me, come! Come to me, come!___ With your haunt-ing, haunt-ing

call.___

What are the tune-ful voi-ces That a-wake at ear-ly dawn? Do they come from the or - ient por - tals Of the Pa lace of — the Morn?

the Pa-lace of the Morn. — They

Andante

tell of a gol - den Ci - ty, With pearl and jas - per

bright,   And of shi - ning forms that beck - on   From the

fair   and ho - ly   light.   Then a

rush   of far - off   harp - ings,   Blends with the vi - sion

Lyrics:
clear, And I know that the night is pass-ing, And I know that the day_ is_ near! I know the day is near!_ I hear_ you, I hear you, Sweet voi-ces of the

dawn! ___ Come to me, come! Come to me, come! ___ In the

ear - ly, ear - ly morn. ___

The Children's Triumph

Words and Music by
Frances Ridley Havergal

The Sun - beams came to my win - dow, And said,__ Come out and

see__ The spar - kle on__ the ri - ver, The blos - som on the tree!_____ Come out_____ Come out and see The blos - som on the

tree_____ But ne-ver a mo-ment par-leyed I With the bright haired Sun-beams'

call;_____ Though their dazz-ling hands on the leaf they laid, I drew it a-way to the cur - tain shade, Where the Sun - beams could not fall.

The Ro - bins came to my

win - dow, And said, Come out and sing! Come out and join the cho - rus Of the Fes - ti-val of Spring_____ Come out_____ Come

out and sing In the Fes - ti-val of Spring!_____ But ne ver a ca - rol

would I trill In the Fes - ti-val of May;_____ But I sat a - lone in my sha - dowy room, And worked a - way in its qui - et gloom, And the Ro-bins flew a-

way.___

The Chil - dren came to my win - dow And said,___ Come out and play!___ Come out with us in the sun - shine, 'Tis such a glo - rious

day___ Come out___ come out and play! 'Tis such a glo - rious

day___ Then ne ver a - no - ther word I wrote, And my desk was put a-

Ped.   ✳

way!___ When the Chil-dren called me what could I do? The Ro-bins failed and the

Sun - beams too, But the Chil - dren, the Chil - dren, the Chil - dren won the

day!___ They won___ they won the day, the Chil - dren won the day.____ They won____ they won the day, The Chil - dren won__ the

day.____

Summer

Words and Music by
Frances Ridley Havergal

What will the sum - mer bring? Sun-shine and

flow'rs,   Bright-ness and me - lo - dy,   Gol - den voiced hours,   Rose gleam-ing morn - ings Vo - cal with praise, Crim - son flush'd eve - nings

Night - in - gale lays. Crim - son flush'd eve - nings Night - in - gale

lays. What will the sum - mer bring? Cool ness and shade, E - lo-quent still-ness In thick-et and glade. Whis-per-ing bree - zes Fra-grance op-

press'd, Lin-ger-ing twi - light Sooth-ing to rest. Come!

Come! Come_ oh come! Sum-mer, bright sum-mer, Sum-mer, bright sum-mer.   Come!   oh,   come.

What will the

sum-mer bring? Glad-ness and mirth,   Bright hours of joy For the chil-dren of

70
earth. Smiles for the old — man Joy for the strong, Glee for the
70
Pno.
76
lit-tle ones All the day long. Glee for the lit-tle ones All the day
76
Pno.
82
pp
long. What will the sum - mer bring? Fresh-ness and calm, To the
82
Pno.
pp

care-worn and trou - bled Beau-ty and balm. O toil wea-ry spi - rit

Rest thee a - new, For the heat of the world - race, Sum-mer hath dew.

Come!   Come!   come_ oh come! Sum-mer bright sum-mer,

Sum-mer bright sum-mer Come! oh come.

Sunset
Vocal Duet

Words by unknown author
Music by Frances Ridley Havergal

First Voice

The

hours of the day are o - ver, and soft - ly the sea - son of

molto legato

light   Goes   out   in a gol - den   glo -   ry,   and

fades from our ra - vish'd   sight.

Second Voice
a tempo

Eve is the sea-son of   rest,   the   sea-son of thought and re - pose,   The o - ver wrought wor-kers hail it, The he-rald of balm for their woes.

Beau-ti - ful gates of the sun - set, or-nate with crim-son and gold. Like the

Beau-ti - ful gates of the sun - set, or-nate with crim-son and gold Like the ta-pes-tried tent of a mo-narch, their bars of pearl un-fold.

ta-pes-tried tent of a mo-narch, their bars of pearl un-fold.

Pno.

Far up in heav'n they o - pen, Bid - ding earth's light grow

Glo - ry to Thee my God this night, For all the

Pno.

dim, ___ That the chil - dren of men may ga - ther, And

bless - ings of the light; Keep me, Oh keep me, King of

Pno.

sing their eve - ning hymn, their eve - ning hymn.

kings, Be - neath Thine own Al - might - y wings.

Pno.

Home - ward! I hear it whis-per'd, whis - per'd,

Home - ward! I hear it whis-per'd, On each dy-ing breath of the

Pno.

whis - per'd, whis - per'd! The bur - den of the sun - set, With its

breeze, 'Tis the bur - den of the sun - set, With its

Pno.

Vocal text, measures 49–51 (upper staff): cho - ral sym - pho - nies. Praise God from

Vocal text, measures 49–51 (lower staff): cho - ral sym - pho - nies._____ Ev - 'ry night__ brings__ us__

Vocal text, measures 52–54 (upper staff): whom all bless - ings flow, Praise Him all crea - tures here be-

Vocal text, measures 52–54 (lower staff): near - er,__ near - er, and ev - 'ry de - part - ing__ sun... __ Bids us__ take__

55
low; Praise Him a - bove ye heav'n - ly host, Praise Fa - ther,
heart and la - bour, and la - bour for soon will our work be
55
Pno.
58
f
Son and Ho - ly Ghost.
f
done, our work be done.
8va
58
Pno.
f

That's Not the Way at Sea

Words and Music by
Frances Ridley Havergal

He stood up-on the fie - ry deck, Our Cap-tain kind and brave! He would not leave the burn-ing wreck While there was one to save. We want-ed him to go be-fore, And we would fol-low fast; We could not bear to leave him there, Be - side the bla-zing

mast, But his voice rang out with a chee-ry shout, And no-ble words spake he That's

not the way at sea, my boys, That's not the way at sea.

So each one did as he was bid, And in-to the boats—we— pass'd, While clos-er came the scorch-ing flame, And our Cap-tain was the last! Yet once a-gain he dar'd his life One lit - tle lad to save; Then we pull'd to shore from the blaze and roar, With our Cap-tain kind and

brave In the face of Death with its fie-ry breath He had stood, and so would

we! For that's the way at sea, my boys, For that's the way at sea.

Now let the no-ble words re-sound, And e-cho far— and— free, Where e-ver Eng-lish hearts are found On Eng-lish shore or sea, The i-ron nerve of du-ty join'd With gol-den vein of

Vocal line lyrics:

love, Can dare to do and dare to wait, With cour-age from a-bove, Our

Cap-tain's shout a-mong the flames, A watch-word long shall be. That's

not the way at sea, my boys, That's not the way at sea.

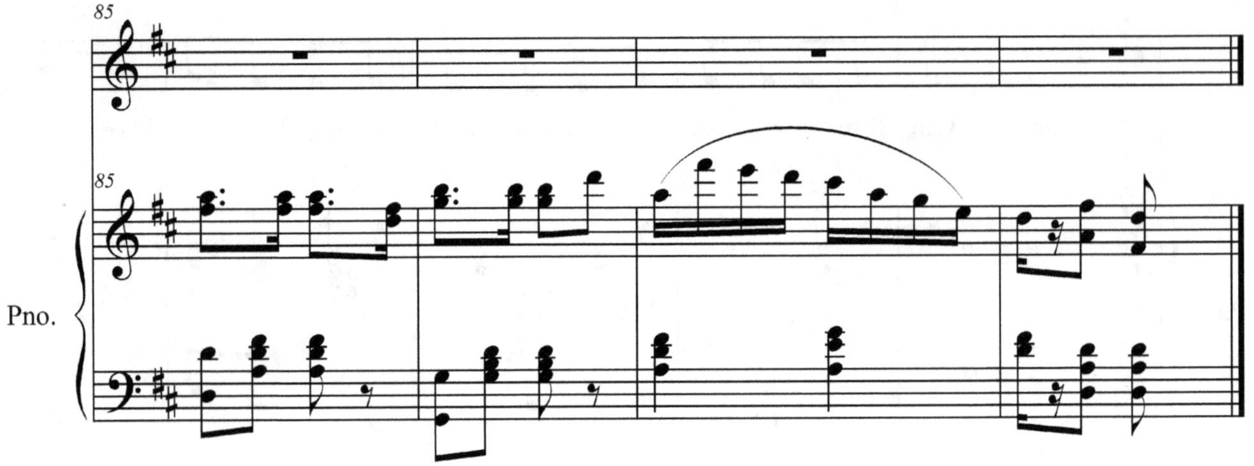
85
85
Pno.

Scotland's Welcome
Song and Chorus

Words and Music by
Frances Ridley Havergal

Sweet Rose of the South!_ con-tent-ed to rest In the fair i-sland

home_ which thy pre-sence has bless'd! From the High-lands re-

F.R.H. wrote in an undated letter, "I am bringing out a Scotch song, "Scotland's Welcome," anent the royal marriage, which I rejoice in—don't you?" This was found in *Letters by the Late Frances Ridley Havergal* edited by her sister Maria Vernon Graham Havergal (London: James Nisbet & Co., 1885), original book page 155, page 190 of Volume IV of the Havergal edition. (The word "anent" means "about, concerning, regarding.") This was the marriage in 1871 of Queen Victoria's daughter Princess Louise to John Campbell, 9th Duke of Argyll and Member of Parliament for Argyllshire in Scotland. They married on March 21, 1871, the first time that an English Princess married a commoner since 1515.

sound - ing glad wel - come shall float, And the Low - lands re-

- ech-o the ju - bi-lant note. Mer ry Eng-land has

loved thee and — cher-ish'd thee long, Her — bles sings go with thee in prayer and in song; Bon-nie Scot-land has won thee, and lays at thy

feet. Love— ten-der and fer-vent, love loy-al and sweet.

Chorus

Our own— bon-nie Scot - land with wel - come shall

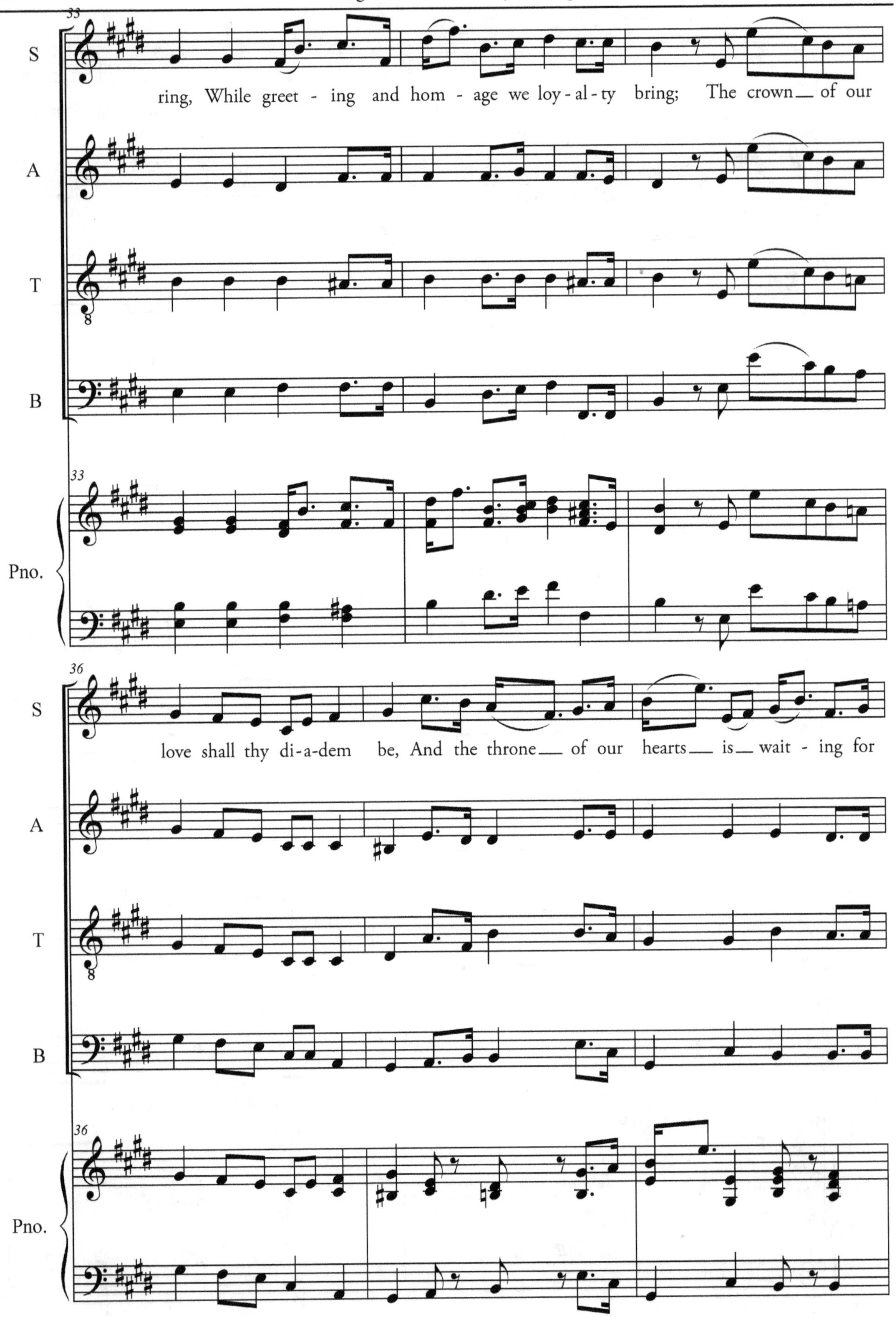
33
S
ring, While greet - ing and hom - age we loy - al - ty bring; The crown of our
A
T
B
33
Pno.
36
S
love shall thy di - a - dem be, And the throne of our hearts is wait - ing for
A
T
B
36
Pno.

Thy crown,___ thy throne,___ are wait-ing for thee.

Then come, like the sun - rise that wakes___ with a

smile   The dark moun - tains   and   val - leys of lone - ly Ar-

gyle,   Gol - den splen - dour shall   fall   on   the   pale __ north - ern

snow, And with rose - light of love __ the __ pur - ple shall   glow.

Tenderly

Though the voice that should bless, and the__ hand that should seal, Is "a - way" and at rest in the "land o' the leal;" May the God of thy fa-ther look gra-cious-ly down, With__ bles-sings on bles sings thy

67
rall.
a tempo
glad - ness to crown!
Chorus
S
Our own bon - nie
A
T
B
Pno.
rall.
a tempo

Scot-land with wel - come shall ring, While greet - ing and hom - age we loy-al-ty

bring; The crown — of our love shall thy di-a-dem be, And the throne — of our hearts ___ is ___ wait - ing for thee. Thy crown, ___ thy throne, ___ are wait-ing for

thee.

The Pilgrims' Song.

Composed by

Frances Ridley Havergal.

Ent. Sta. Hall.

Price 3/-

Published by
HUTCHINGS & ROMER,
LONDON.
W.

IN E MINOR.
FOR CONTRALTO OR BASS.

IN G MINOR.
FOR MEZZO-SOPRANO OR BARITONE.

LOVING ALL ALONG.

Sacred Song.

WORDS BY

S. Gillespie Prout,

The Music by

FRANCES RIDLEY HAVERGAL.

Ent. Sta. Hall.

Price 3/-

London;
HUTCHINGS & ROMER,
9, CONDUIT STREET, REGENT STREET,

Title pages of two of F.R.H.'s art songs. "Loving all along" was written very late in her life, and the faint initials "F.R.H." were written by another (possibly Maria or another family member) after her death.

Thou Knowest
Sacred Song

Music by Frances Ridley Havergal
Words by Rea [or REA ?]

Yet I have long'd_____ to come, Day af - ter day._____

appassionato

For well my heart has known Bit-ter - est tears;

One day would fall and dim All the vain years, All,_____

All_____ the vain years. Still_____ to the late and sad Mer - - - cy Thou show- est, And how I need it now, Fa - ther, Thou

59
p
know - est, Fa - ther, Thou know - est,
Pno.
p
65
Fa - ther! Fa - ther! Thou, Thou know-
Pno.
Ped.
Ped.
72
rall.
est! Thou know - est, Fa - ther, Thou
Pno.
rall.

know - est!

Wea-ry and

sor - - - row-ful,   Life has no zest,_____ no zest,

And I have come_____ to crave   Par - don and rest._____

Now with my ach-ing hands Striv-ing to cling Close to the

Cross, my griefs All would I bring, All,_____

All_____ would I bring. E'en_____ to earth's

ling - 'ring ones   Mer - - - cy Thou show - est;

Oh!   how   I   need   it   now,   Fa - ther,   Thou know-

est,   Fa - ther,   Thou know - est.   Fa-

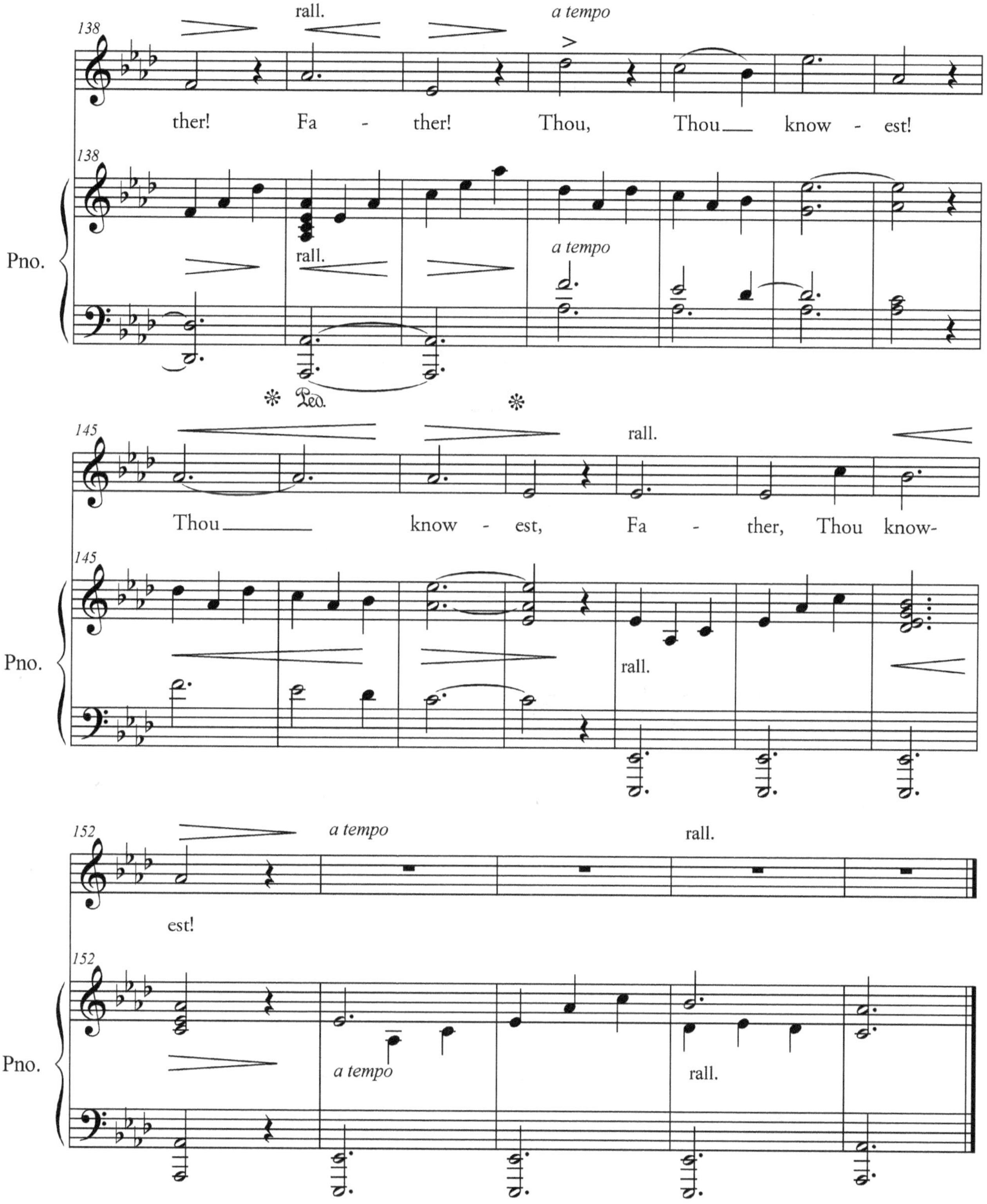

Lyrics (vocal line):

ther!   Fa - ther!   Thou,   Thou___ know - est!

Thou _____ know - est,   Fa - ther,   Thou know-

est!

Thy Father Waits

Words and Music by
Frances Ridley Havergal

1.Wan-d'rer from thy Fa ther's home, So full of sin,___ so far a-

way! Wilt thou a - ny lon - ger roam? Oh, wilt thou

not re-turn to - day? Wilt thou? oh, He knows it all; Thy

Fa-ther sees,_____ He meets thee here, Wilt thou hear His ten - der call? Re - turn! re - turn! while He is near!

Refrain after each verse
He is wait-ing, wait-ing, wait-ing! Thy Fa-ther waits for thee! O

wan - d'ring child, thy Fa - ther waits for thee!

2. He is here! His loving voice

    Hath reached thee, though so far away!

He is waiting to rejoice,

    O wandering one, o'er thee to-day.

Waiting, waiting to bestow

    His perfect pardon, full and free;

Waiting, waiting till thou know

    His wealth of love for thee, for thee!

Refrain: He is waiting, waiting, waiting!

    Thy Father waits for thee!

    O wandering child, thy Father waits for thee!

3. Rise and go! Thy Father waits

    To welcome, and receive, and bless;

Thou shalt tread His palace gates

    In royal robe of righteousness.

Thine shall be His heart of love,

    And thine His smile, and thine His home,

Thine His joy, all joys above:

    O wandering child, no longer roam!

Refrain: He is waiting, waiting, waiting!

    Thy Father waits for thee!

    O wandering child, thy Father waits for thee!

Will Ye Not Come?

"Incline your ear, and come unto Me: hear, and your soul shall live."—Isaiah 55:3.
"Him that cometh to Me I will in no wise cast out."—John 6:37.

Words and Music by
Frances Ridley Havergal

Tune-Lucius

1.Will ye not come to Him for life? Why will ye die?— oh, why?

He gave His life for you! for you! The gift is free, the Word is

true! Will ye not come? oh, why will ye die? Will ye not come? will ye not

Refrain ad lib., after any or each verse

(Measure 12) come? will ye not come to Him? to Him? Oh, come, come, come to

(Measure 16) Him! Come on-to Je-sus, oh come___ to Him!

2. Will ye not come to Him for peace,
   Peace through His cross alone?
   He shed His precious blood for you;
   The gift is free, the word is true!
   He is our Peace, oh is He your own?
   Will ye not come? &c.—for *Peace!*

3. Will ye not come to Him for rest?
   All that are weary, come:
   The rest He gives is deep and true,
   'Tis offered now, 'tis offered you;
   Rest in His love, and rest in His home.
   Will ye not come? &c.—for *Rest!*

4. Will ye not come to Him for joy?
   Will ye not come for this?
   He laid His joys aside for you,
   To give you joy, so sweet, so true!
   Sorrowing heart, oh drink of the bliss!
   Will ye not come? &c.—for *Joy!*

5. Will ye not come to Him for love,
   Love that can fill the heart?
   Exceeding great, exceeding free!
   He loveth you, He loveth me!
   Will you not come? why stand ye apart?
   Will ye not come? &c.—for *Love!*

6. Will ye not come to Him for all?
   Will ye not "taste and see"?
   He waits to give it all to you,
   The gifts are free, the words are true!
   Jesus hath said it, "Come unto Me."
   Will ye not come? &c.—for *All!*

The Lord Hath Done It!

"Sing, O ye heavens; for the Lord hath done it."—Isaiah 44: 23.

Words and Music by
Frances Ridley Havergal

1.Sing, O heav'ns! the Lord hath done it! Sound it forth o'er land and sea! Je - sus says "I have re - deemed thee, Now re - turn, re - turn to Me!" O re - turn! for His own life - blood Paid the ran - som, made us free Ev - er - more__ and e - ver - more!

2.For I know that what He do - eth Stands for e - ver, fixed and true; No - thing can be add - ed to it, No - thing left for us to do. No - thing can be ta - ken from it: Done for me, and done for you E - ver - more__ and e - ver - more!

rall.

3. Listen now! the Lord hath done it!
   For He loved us unto death;
   It is finished, He hath saved us!
   Only trust to what He saith!
   He hath done it, come and bless Him,
   Spend in praise your ransomed breath
   Evermore and evermore!

4. O believe the Lord hath done it!
   Wherefore linger? wherefore doubt?
   All the cloud of black transgression
   He Himself hath blotted out.
   He hath done it, come and bless Him!
   Swell the grand thanksgiving shout
   Evermore and evermore!

God Bless the Boys of England

Music by Frances Ridley Havergal
Words by Rev. Robert Maguire, D. D.

hon - our and suc - cess; O God who art their Fa - ther, The Boys of England

bless! The Boys of Eng - land bless, The Boys of Eng - land

24
a tempo
bless!
Chorus
S
Oh, bless the Boys of Eng - land! The Boys of Eng land bless! The
A
Oh, bless the Boys of Eng - land! The Boys of Eng land bless! The
B
Oh, bless the Boys of Eng - land! The Boys of Eng land bless! oh bless! The
24
Pno.
a tempo

29 D.C. verses 1, 3, and 5

God

S: Boys of Eng-land bless, The Boys of Eng-land bless!

A: Boys of Eng-land bless, The Boys of Eng-land bless!

B: Boys of Eng-land bless, The Boys of Eng-land bless!

33 Verses 2, 4, and 6

bless the Boys of Eng - land, Our fu-ture men to be, Our Sai-lors and our

Sol - diers, To serve on land or sea! Our mer - chants and our

tra - ders To co - ver all the earth, To bless by their ex-

am - ple The coun - try of their birth, The coun - try of their

2. God bless the Boys of England,
     Our future men to be,
  Our sailors and our soldiers,
     To serve on land and sea;
  Our merchants and our traders,
     To cover all the earth,
  To bless by their example
     The country of their birth.
Chorus. Three Voices.
     God bless the Boys of England,…The
     country of their birth.

3. God bless the Boys of England,
     That, like Thy Holy Child,
  Who grew in years and favour,
     All pure and undefiled,
  They, as they grow in stature,
     May walk in wisdom's ways,
  Rejoicing in Thy favour,
     And happy all their days.
Chorus. Three Voices.
     Oh, bless the Boys of England!…The
     Boys of England bless!

4. God bless the Boys of England,
     The homes in which they dwell,
  The schools of their up-bringing,
     The Church they love so well;
  Their fathers and their mothers,
     The friends that help them on;
  Bless all that shew them kindness,
     Bless all the kindness shown.
Chorus. Three Voices.
     God bless the Boys of England,…The
     country of their birth.

5. God bless the Boys of England,
     Their hearts and tongues employ,
  To carry to the nations
     "Good tidings of great joy:"
  Beneath the Gospel banner,
     For victory unfurled,
  To win men's hearts to Jesus,
     The Saviour of the world.
Chorus. Three Voices.
     Oh, bless the Boys of England!…The
     Boys of England bless!

6. God bless the Boys of England,
     The Boys and Maidens bless;
  Grant all that may be needful,
     For life and godliness;
  The Boys of happy England,
     Bless them at home, abroad;
  God bless the Boys and Maidens,
     O God, our fathers' God !
Chorus. Three Voices.
     God bless the Boys of England,…The country of their birth

The Good Old Church of England

Music by Frances Ridley Havergal
Words by Rev. W. Blake Atkinson

1. The good old Church of Eng - land! A thou - sand years __ have fled Since first u - pon our is - land home Thy lamp its lus - tre shed. What e - ver ad - verse winds might blow, 'Twas lit by ho - ly men, And God has kept a - live till now The flame __ they kin - dled then.

2. The good old Church of Eng - land! Be - neath the sway __ of time Thy roots have reached to ma - ny lands, And spread in ev - 'ry clime; Till, far a - round as eye can see, A good - ly grove ap - pears, Where high the pa - tri - arch - al tree Its state - ly crown up - rears.

3. The good old Church of England!
   Though foes without assail,
   And hidden danger threatens thee
   From some within thy pale—
   Still, still, by stores unfailing fed,
   And kept by bulwarks strong,
   The conqueror's train shall never tread
   Thine ancient streets along.

4. The good old Church of England!
   No wave shall thee o'erwhelm:
   We trust a mightier Hand than ours
   Is laid upon thy helm;
   That, safely steered through storm and tide,
   The foaming breakers past,
   Thy weather-beaten hull shall ride
   Within the port at last.

5. The good old Church of England!
   A faithful guide be thou
   Amid the dangers and the doubts
   That crowd around us now.
   True to the simple Gospel word,
   Lead on thy pilgrim band,
   Till their glad eyes behold their Lord
   And greet the promised land.

6. The good old Church of England!
   Founded upon a rock,
   May strength Divine preserve thy fold
   Secure from every shock;
   Till the great Shepherd of the sheep
   In clouds of glory come,
   His flocks on earth to take and keep
   In one Eternal Home.

O'er the Plains
A Christmas Carol

Verse 1-Repeating for second half

Andante maetoso

Music by Frances Ridley Havergal
Words by Rev. W. J. Vernon, B. A.

1.O'er the plains the dark-ness deep-ens, Shades of night, a-bove, be-
Faith and Hope, at-tent, are watch-ing For the to-kens of the

low;— All a-round a gloo-my si-lence
morn;— Through the chill night air is glow-ing

Allegro spiritoso

Speaks a world of sin and woe;— 2.Like a
Love, be-liev-ing, yet for-lorn.

slum b'rer waked by sun light, See the sleep ing world a - rise! O the__ sud den blaze of

glo - ry Burst - ing on the dark-ened eyes! Light of Light, the Fa - ther's

Bright ness, Sun of Right eous-ness is nigh,— And the__ shades of night for-

e - ver Van - ish in His Light, and die. A - men.

3. Hark! what music fills the Heavens,
    Chanted by celestial choirs!
From the deep unseen resounding,
    Echoing to seraphic lyres!
Rapt in solemn awe, adoring
    Three in One and One in Three,—
All Creation wonders, listening
    To the Angels' minstrelsy.

4. "Glory to the King Eternal!
    Maker, Father, Friend of Man!
Ruler of the Hosts of Heaven,
    Framer of the wondrous plan;—
Glory to the Son Incarnate!
    Stooping to the world He made—
Mighty Monarch! robed in glory!
    Babe in lowly manger laid!

5. "Glory to the Spirit moving
    O'er the void and darkened waste,—
Light and Life He gives to sinners,
    By the primal sin abased;—
Glory to Jehovah Jesus!
    Glory to the Three in One!
Hallelujah! God is Human,
    Man Divine, in God's own Son!

6. "Hail! ye mortals! captive, blinded,
    Straying, wandering, dying, dead,—
Yours are freedom, truth, and guidance,
    God's own Light is on you shed!
Peace and Mercy, Life and Glory,
    All are yours, in God who dwell;—
God is Love! He comes to give you
    His own self, Emmanuel!

7. "Hail! immortal heirs of Glory!
    Citizens of Heaven above!
God in Man is in yon manger,—
    Cradled there, Eternal Love!
Babe of Bethlehem! We know Thee,
    Dying, Risen, Ascended Lord!
Mighty God! Triumphant Victor!
    By angelic Hosts adored!"

8. Glory to the Eternal Father!
    To the Incarnate Son, we sing!
Glory to the Spirit dwelling
    In the hearts where Christ is King—
Glory to Jehovah Jesus!
    Glory to the Three in One!
Hallelujah! God is Human,
    Man Divine, in God's own Son!

Worthy the Lamb
Sacred Song

Music by Frances Ridley Havergal
Words by John Kent

Tune-Euodias

1.'Tis the church tri - um - phant sing - ing. Wor - thy the Lamb!
3.Harps and songs for - e - ver sound - ing, Wor - thy the Lamb!
4.Sing with blest an - ti - ci - pa - tion Wor - thy the Lamb!

Heav'n through - out with prais - es ring - ing, Wor - thy the
Migh - ty grace o'er sin a - bound - ing, Wor - thy the
Thro' the vale of tri - bu - la - tion, Wor - thy the

12

Lamb!   Thrones and pow'rs be - fore Him bend - ing,
Lamb!   By   His blood He dear - ly bought us;
Lamb!   Sweet - est notes, all   notes ex - cel - ling,

15

O - dours sweet with voice as - cend - ing, Swell the cho - rus   ne - ver end - ing,
Wand - 'ring from the   fold He sought us,   And to glo - ry   safe - ly brought us,
On   the theme for - e - ver dwel - ling, Still un - told, though e - ver tell - ing,

19

Wor - thy the Lamb,   Wor - thy the Lamb!
Wor - thy the Lamb,   Wor - thy the Lamb!
Wor - thy the Lamb,   Wor - thy the Lamb!

Fine
2.Ev - 'ry kin - dred, tongue and na - tion,
Pno.
(8va)
Fine
Ped.
Wor - thy the Lamb! Join to sing the great sal - va - tion, Wor - thy the
Pno.
Ped.
Lamb! Loud as migh - ty thun - ders roar - ing,
Pno.

Floods   of migh - ty   wa - ters   pour - ing,   Pros-trate at His

feet a - dor - ing,   Wor - thy   the   Lamb!   Wor - thy   the

D.S. al Fine

Lamb!

D.S. al Fine

Begin at Once!

Her Last Message, May 23rd 1879

To those who have signed,
"Behold God HImself is with us for our Captain,"—2 Chron. 13: 12.
To those who have not signed,
"Come thou with us, and we will do thee good."—Numbers 10: 29.

Words and Music by
Frances Ridley Havergal

1.Be - gin at once! In the plea - sant days, While we are all___ to - ge - ther,
2.Be - gin at once! For we do not know What may be - fall___ to - mor - row!

While we can meet for prayer___ and praise, While we can join in
Ma - ny a temp - ter, ma - ny a foe, Li - eth in wait where

health - ful plays,   In the   glow___ of sum - mer   wea - ther. Be - gin   at once with
'er___ we   go   With the   snare___ that leads   to   sor - row. Be - gin   at once! nor

heart and hand,   And   swell   the   ranks___   And   swell___   the   ranks___   the
doubt - ing stand   But   swell   the   ranks___   But   swell___   the   ranks___   the

ranks   of our hap - py   band!___
ranks   of our hap - py   band!___

3.Be - gin   at once! There is
4.Be - gin   at once! In the

much to do; O do not wait for o-thers! Join us to-day, be
strength of God, For that will ne-ver fail you! Un-der His ban-ner,

brave and true! Join us to-day there's room for you, And a
bright and broad, You shall be safe from fear and fraud And from

wel-come from your bro-thers, Be-gin at once! The work is grand That
all that can as-sail you, Be-gin at once! with re-so-lute stand. And

God   has   giv'n,_____ That   God _____ has   giv'n,_____ has
swell   the   ranks,_____ And   swell _____ the   ranks,_____ the

giv'n   to our hap - py   band._____
ranks   of our hap - py   band._____

Safe Home

Music by unknown composer,
possibly by Frances Ridley Havergal
Words by Barbara Miller McAndrew

'Twas the shin-ing ci-ty's por - tals, And the pear-ly gates a-far Shone bright with Je-ho-vah's glo - ry As at eve the ves - per star. And the streets of gold were

sound - ing, With glad notes of rap - ture long For

white - robed hosts were wel - com - ing To Heav'n a ran - somed

2. And who were those they welcomed,
    And what was the song they sang?
  For the jasper walls resounded,
    And heaven's wide arches rang.
  No kings of the earth were coming,
    And they were not men of age;
  But those who gave their hearts to God
    In their life's young pilgrimage.

3. The pilgrims entered the city,
    Like worn sky-birds to their nest;
  Where the wicked cease from troubling,
    And the weary are at rest.
  And each one swept a golden harp,
    And raised a rapturous lay,
  And Jesus gave to each a crown
    Which shall ne'er fade away.

This is one of three manuscript scores, or at least hand-copied scores, of "Safe Home" found among Havergal manuscripts and papers. One of the scores has a front cover page with only the title "Safe Home" and at the very top edge of the page a barely readable "M. V. G. Havergal." Frances' sister Maria was a trained musician, and possibly she composed this score; also very possibly the name only meant that she copied out that score or that the score should be returned to her. Very possibly F.R.H. composed this. We don't know. At the top of each of the three copies, neither the name of the poet nor of the composer is given.

Index to First Lines

"Confidence" was written on September 26, 1870, and was later given the sub-title "Impromptu on the road to Warwick." In this manuscript in F.R.H.'s handwriting, she assigned this to be set to Handel's score, an Air sung by Susanna in Act Two, Scene 4, of Handel's Oratorio Susanna. *Frances was likely the one who made this arrangement published by Huthchings & Romer.*

F. A. S.

In Thee I Trust,

Sacred Song,

WORDS BY

FRANCES RIDLEY HAVERGAL,

COMPOSED

BY

Handel.

Ent. Sta. Hall.   Price 3/-

PUBLISHED BY
HUTCHINGS & ROMER,
LONDON,
W.

In Thee I Trust

Sacred Song

Music by Georg Friedrich Handel
Words by Frances Ridley Havergal

In Thee I trust,

on Thee I rest, O Sa - viour dear, O Sa - viour dear, Re-

deem - er blest! No earth - ly friend, no bro - ther knows

My wear - i - ness, ___ my wants, ___ my woes; In ___ Thee a - lone

I seek re - pose.   O Sa - viour dear,   Re - deem - er blest,   In Thee I ___

trust,   In Thee I ___ trust,   on   Thee I ___ rest.

Thy pow'r, Thy love, Thy faith-ful - ness,

With lip and — life, With lip and — life I long — to — bless. Thy

faith - ful - ness shall be my tower. My sun Thy love, — my

shield__ Thy pow'r, In__ deep - est grief, in dark - est__ hour.

O Sa - viour dear, Re - deem - er blest! In Thee I__ trust, In Thee I__

trust, on Thee I__ rest.

IN B FLAT.
Contralto.

TO
CONSTANCE FLINDT.

IN D.
Soprano.

"ENOUGH,"

Sacred Song,

WORDS BY

FRANCES RIDLEY HAVERGAL,

Music by

FRANCESCO BERGER.

Ent. Sta. Hall.

Price 3/=

London,
LAMBORN COCK, 63, NEW BOND STREET.

Also by the same
SACRED SONG, "JESUS ONLY." 3

F.R.H. wrote this in a letter, likely written in 1876 [1]: "Francesco Berger has lately made a *very* beautiful song of my words, 'Enough.' This is published by Lamborn & Cocks, London; and I greatly hope it will circulate, for the sake of setting forth the truth of the words."

[1] *Letters by the Late Frances Ridley Havergal* (London : James Nisbet & Co., 1886), page 251. See page 215 of Volume IV of the Havergal edition. The complete poem "Enough" is found on page 110 of this volume.

Enough

Words by Frances Ridley Havergal
Music by Francesco Berger

Andante, non troppo Adagio

I am so weak, dear Lord!   I can-not stand One   mo-ment with-out Thee,   One

mo - ment with - out Thee;   But   oh!   the ten - der - ness_____

Sop.
Pno.
cresc.
— of Thine en - fold - ing, And oh! the faith - ful - ness
cresc.
— of Thine up - hold - ing, And oh! the strength of
f
f
Thy right hand! That strength is e-nough for me, That
f
f

17
rit.
a tempo
Sop.
strength is e-nough for me!
Pno.
rit.
a tempo
f
21
p
I am so nee-dy, Lord! and yet I know All
f
p
dolcissin
rall.
pp
25
ful - ness dwells in Thee, All ful - ness dwells in Thee; And
rall.

Sop.
Pno.
cresc.
hour by hour that ne-ver fail-ing trea-sure Sup - ports, and fills, in
pp
cresc.
o-ver flow-ing mea-sure, My least, my great - est need, and so: Thy
f
grace is e-nough for me, Thy grace is e-nough for me.
rit.
a tempo

There were strange soul-depths, rest-less, vast, and broad,

Un - fathom-èd as the sea; An in-fi-nite___ cra-ving for

47
Sop.
Pno.
f allargando
some in-fi-nite still-ing; But now Thy per - fect love is per - fect
f allargando
50
f grandioso
f
fill-ing! Lord Je - sus Christ, my Lord, my
f grandioso
f
54
f allargando
f ritard molto
God, Thou, Thou art e - nough for me, Thou art e-nough for
f allargando
f ritard molto

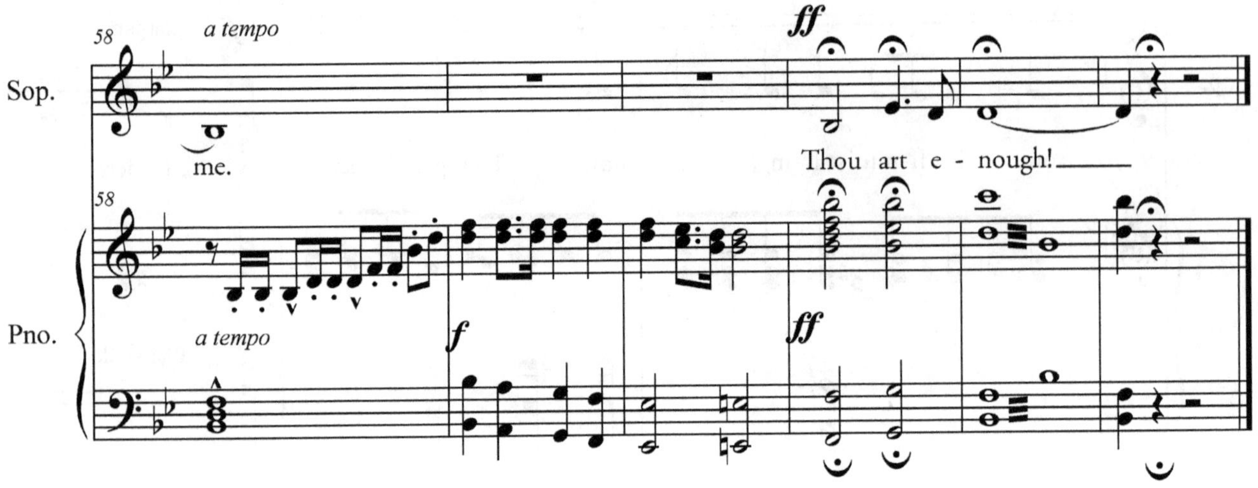
58
a tempo
Sop.
me.
ff
Thou art e - nough!
Pno.
a tempo
f
ff